More Praise for *A Teacher's Gui*

"Reading *The Go-Giver* not only changed my thinking; a[s part of] a city-wide book club, it changed the thinking of our entire community. By focusing on the principles contained in *The Go-Giver* with intentionality, positivity abounds."
—Andy Mack, mayor, Longview, Texas

"When the first edition of *The Go-Giver* was published in 2007, I started using it with my advanced leadership college group at our annual retreat. While this new *Teacher's Guide to The Go-Giver* was originally developed for high school teachers, there are many pearls throughout that college professors can use with their students, too. The core concept discussion questions, quick writing and group discussion suggestions, and critical thinking questions all provide rich ideas for engaging college students around the concepts in *The Go-Giver*. The final project suggestions will stimulate possibilities for more in-depth integration of *The Go-Giver* concepts into our students' everyday lives. As educators, we ultimately are called improve the world through our students. *The Go-Giver* and this *Teacher's Guide* will assist us in that noble calling!"
— Tim O. Peterson, Ph.D., associate dean and professor of management, North Dakota State University

"In our seminar for juniors and seniors in the College of Business at Colorado State University we use *The Go-Giver* to help create in our students a sense of individual self-efficacy, personal leadership, and the understanding that they can lead immediately. Everything we do in the seminar fits the words from Lesson One of this *Teacher's Guide*: 'How can I model these lessons in my life?'"
— William Shuster, MBA, professor of management, Colorado State University

"I have known Randy Stelter for over forty years and have closely followed his extraordinary teaching and coaching career. In this *Teacher's Guide* he makes the concepts in *The Go-Giver* become a reality in the students' lives. I plan to teach *The Go-Giver* in my leadership class at the University of St. Francis, and I know this *Guide* will greatly enhance my teaching."
— Pat Sullivan, professor and former head basketball coach, University of St. Francis, Joliet, Illinois

"While I am not a teacher per se, I use the principles in *The Go-Giver* every day in interactions with my children, my patients, and my employees. As parents, doctors, and leaders, we are all first teachers. I am impressed with the way this *Teacher's Guide* approaches the concepts of the book through critical thinking. By igniting our youth and teaching our children through these concepts, we empower them to create positive change in the world while achieving great things. This book is not just for teachers, it's for *everyone*."
— Kelli Winarksi, B.A., D.C., Family First Chiropractic and Wellness Center, Columbia, Missouri

Praise for *The Go-Giver*

"*The Go-Giver* is the most important parable about business—and life—of our time."
— Adam Grant, Wharton professor, author of *Give and Take*

"Giving, touching others' lives, expanding the circle of our concern to include others, being authentic and being always open to receiving as well as giving. That's not just a children's fairy tale—it's a good description of many of the most amazing people I've encountered."
—Arianna Huffington, founder of *Huffington Post* (from her foreword to *The Go-Giver*)

"*The Go-Giver* is a must-read for anyone who wants to change the world."
—Glenn Beck, talk show host and founder of *TheBlaze*

"*The Go-Giver* is a small book that packs a huge idea. The surest path to success—in all senses of that overused word—is to give. As Burg and Mann show in their compelling tale, not only do givers prosper, they also change the world."
—Daniel H. Pink, author of *To Sell Is Human* and *Drive*

"*The Go-Giver* is one of my favorite books ever. It has made a huge difference in my life, and it aligns with everything I stand for."
—Marie Forleo, founder of B-School and MarieTV

"Deeply heartfelt and meditative, *The Go-Giver* is filled with insights. More important, it accomplishes what few business books do—it reminds us of our own core humanity."
—Ori Brafman, coauthor of *The Starfish and the Spider*, *Sway*, and *Click*

"*The Go-Giver* is filled with timeless truths practically presented that will positively transform every reader; it's a brilliant and easily read guide to doing good and doing well."
—Rabbi Daniel Lapin, author of *Business Secrets from the Bible* and *Thou Shall Prosper*

"*The Go-Giver* should be handed out to every new college student as required reading."
—Angela Loehr Chrysler, CEO of Team National, Inc., director of National Companies, Inc.

"The world always needs a fresh approach to its most important messages. *The Go-Giver* is a great way to spread a positive and enriching message."
—Soundview Executive Book Alert

A Teacher's Guide to
The Go-Giver

A Curriculum for Making a Difference

Randy Stelter, Bob Burg and John David Mann

Copyright © 2015 by Randy Stelter, Bob Burg and John David Mann

All rights reserved, including the right of reproduction in whole or in part in any form. The reproduction and distribution of the material in this guide via the Internet or any other means without the express permission of the authors is illegal. Your support of the authors' rights is appreciated.

Published by Go-Givers International LLC
www.thegogiver.com/guide

ISBN 978-0-9970758-0-9
Library of Congress Control Number: 2015960366
Printed in the United States of America
Set in Apollo MT Std and Aperto

The Go-Giver: A Little Story About a Powerful Business Idea is published by Portfolio/Penguin, an imprint of Penguin Random House LLC.

About the Book

T*he Go-Giver* tells the story of an ambitious young man named Joe who yearns for success. Joe is a true go-getter, but is frustrated: sometimes he feels as if the harder he works, the further away his goals seem to be. Desperate to land a key sale at the end of a bad quarter, he seeks advice from a legendary and enigmatic consultant named Pindar, who introduces Joe to a series of "go-givers" and shows him his Trade Secret, in the form of five "Laws of Stratospheric Success."

In the course of one week, Joe learns that changing his focus from *getting* to *giving*—putting others' interests first and continually adding value to their lives—ultimately leads to unexpected rewards.

In the years since *The Go-Giver*'s publication, the term "go-giver" has become shorthand for a defining set of values embraced by hundreds of thousands of people around the world, helping them find fulfillment *and* greater success in business, in their personal lives and in their communities.

About This Guide

Originally intended for adult readers, especially in the business community, *The Go-Giver* touched a chord in people from all walks of life—including avid young readers, from middle school through college age.

Shortly after its publication the book was picked up by Randy Stelter, an English teacher and athletic director in the northwest Indiana school system, and adopted as a core part of the curriculum for their reading resources program, designed to enhance students' perspective on "what it's going to take to be successful in the real world." Randy has taken Wheeler's senior class through the book every year from 2009 through the present. Soon other educators began following suit, adopting the book as part of their curricula at every level from high school through graduate school.

What follows is an educator's guide for using *The Go-Giver* as part of a curriculum designed for high school students; it can also be adapted for use in higher-education settings.

Randy Stelter
Bob Burg
John David Mann

Contents

ABOUT THE BOOK / ABOUT THIS GUIDE iii

HOW TO USE THIS CURRICULUM GUIDE 1

THE FIVE LAWS OF STRATOSPHERIC SUCCESS (from *The Go-Giver*) 5

LESSON ONE 7
    Core concept discussion: What is *success*?
    Introduce word lists
    Introduce character guides
    Assigned reading: chapters 1–2
    Review vocabulary and characters
    Questions for comprehension
    Going deeper: questions for critical thinking

Lesson One work sheets 11

LESSON TWO 17
    Core concept discussion: What is *value*?
    Preparation: word list, character guide, and Five Laws journal
    Assigned reading: chapters 3–4
    Review vocabulary and characters
    Questions for comprehension
    Going deeper: questions for critical thinking
    Five Laws journal discussion

Lesson Two work sheets 20

LESSON THREE 25
    Core concept discussion: What is *service*?
    Preparation: word list, character guide, and Five Laws journal
    Assigned reading: chapters 5–7
    Review vocabulary and characters
    Questions for comprehension

Going deeper: questions for critical thinking
  Five Laws journal discussion
 Lesson Three work sheets 28

 LESSON FOUR 33
  Core concept discussion: What is *influence*?
  Preparation: word list, character guide, and Five Laws journal
  Assigned reading: chapters 8–9
  Review vocabulary and characters
  Questions for comprehension
  Going deeper: questions for critical thinking
  Five Laws journal discussion
 Lesson Four work sheets 36

 LESSON FIVE 41
  Core concept discussion: What does it mean to be *authentic*?
  Preparation: word list, character guide, and Five Laws journal
  Assigned reading: chapters 10–11
  Review vocabulary and characters
  Questions for comprehension
  Going deeper: questions for critical thinking
  Five Laws journal discussion
 Lesson Five work sheets 44

 LESSON SIX 47
  Core concept discussion: What is the connection between *giving* and *receiving*?
  Preparation: word list, character guide, and Five Laws journal
  Assigned reading: chapters 12–13
  Review vocabulary and characters
  Questions for comprehension
  Going deeper: questions for critical thinking
  Five Laws journal discussion
 Lesson Six works sheets 50

 LESSON SEVEN 53
  Core concept discussion: What is *success*?
  Preparation: word list and character guide

    Assigned reading: chapter 14, Foreword and Introduction
    Review vocabulary and characters
    Questions for comprehension
    Going deeper: questions for critical thinking
    Five Laws journal discussion
Lesson Seven work sheets 56

FINAL PROJECTS 61

Resources   63
Thanks   65
About the Authors   66

How to Use This Curriculum Guide

The lessons in this curriculum are structured in three parts: 1) preliminary discussion of a core concept and preparation for reading—vocabulary, a character guide, and in some lessons a Five Laws journal; 2) an assigned reading from the book; and 3) questions and activities following the reading for review, comprehension, critical thinking, and personal application.

Core Concept Discussion

Each lesson begins with in-class discussion of one core concept from that lesson's assigned reading. The objective is to set the student's purpose for reading and stimulate their thought process about how the core concepts of the book might apply in their own lives.

Preparation: Word List

Each lesson's vocabulary is introduced prior to reading that lesson's selection, with varied activities to help them learn and absorb these words. These activities might include:
- Define the vocabulary using a graphic organizer, notebook, or three-ring binder.
- Identify each word's syntactic function (parts of speech).
- Identify each word's Greek/Latin roots. The more exposure we can give our students to affixes and root word meanings, the better prepared they will be to decode unfamiliar words and their meanings. This will also help them on their SATs, ACTs, and other standardized tests.

Preparation: Character Guide

The character guides pose a series of five questions for each major character as he or she is introduced into the story. Encourage the students to keep these guides and come back to them as they go through later lessons, adding any new insights they gain into that character as the story progresses. The objective is to deepen students' comprehension as they read and help make them aware of the authors' use and methods of characterization.

Preparation: Five Laws Journal

There are five journal pages, one for each of the Five Laws of Stratospheric Success from the book. Each journal page provides a space for the student to write out the wording of that law (writing it themselves aids memorization and increases comprehension), and a lined page for dated entries answering the question, "How did I apply this law today?"

The objective here is to have students actively look for ways to apply insights from the book in their own lives, moving their reading experience from theoretical and abstract to practical and personal. Encourage students to look for little ways to apply each law. Sometimes it is the little gestures that end up making a big difference. (This certainly is what happens to Joe in the book!)

Although each law is explored in one specific lesson, encourage the students to continue working with each existing law even as they add new ones, going back to their journal pages and adding fresh entries throughout the course.

Assigned Reading

The text used for this curriculum is the 2015 "Expanded Edition" version of the book, not the original 2007 edition. This is important; page numbers given in the word lists do not correspond accurately to the 2007 edition, and there are supplemental materials (foreword and introduction) used as part of lesson seven that do not appear in the 2007 edition. Sources for bulk purchase at discount rates are provided on the Resources page.

Review: Vocabulary

In-class review of the vocabulary from that lesson's word list might include:

- Have students write a short story, poem, or brief essay using the vocabulary words in context to show comprehension.
- Create quizzes to test students' understanding of and ability to use these words.
- Create crosswords using that lesson's words.
- Create games around those words. For example, Randy Stelter has led his students in a Jeopardy-style game, with the class divided into teams and playing for points; and Vocabulary Football, where each team gets four chances to correctly define a word or the other team intercepts and takes the "ball."

Review: Characters

Review of the characters introduced in the reading typically begins with discussion, either in small groups or in the class as a whole, of the questions from that lesson's character guide. It also might include additional questions, given out for discussion or essay, such as:

- What positive traits does each character bring to the table?
- Which character in this reading is most like you?
- Which character had the most impact on you?
- Which character do you respect the most, and why?
- If you could meet just one character face to face, whom would it be and why?

Questions for Comprehension

The *Teacher's Guide* offers a set of questions for comprehension following each reading assignment. These can be given out for discussion in small groups, or as part of whole-class discussion. Another option is to give the questions out first as a quiz, and then, after the students have written their own answers, open the questions up to discussion.

Going Deeper: Questions for Critical Thinking

Questions and topics for critical thinking and deeper exploration are offered as a set of writing exercises.

Five Laws Journal Discussion

The Five Laws of Stratospheric Success that Pindar and his friends show Joe in the book articulate the five core ideas in *The Go-Giver*. In the story, Pindar gives Joe one condition he is required to fulfill for their meetings to continue: that he test each law he learns by actually applying it in his life, right away, the same day he learns it.

The purpose of the Five Laws journal work sheets is to encourage students to do exactly as Joe does, and actively apply the key lessons of their reading in their own lives. Prior to each assigned reading, let students know they should come to class prepared to share ways they found to apply that lesson's law.

Final Projects and Final Exam

In teaching *The Go-Giver* at Wheeler High, Randy does not give a final exam per se. Instead, he assigns a final project toward the end of the session to give his students an opportunity to deepen their understanding of the book and to ground its lessons in their own experience. A dozen sample projects are provided in this *Guide*.

Beyond that, the students' "final exam" is to go out and put the Five Laws of Stratospheric Success into action in their own lives and careers.

Work Sheet PDFs

The work sheets (word lists, character guides, and Five Laws journals) for each lesson are provided here at the end of each lesson. We have also made the complete set available as a separate PDF file, available at no cost to anyone who has purchased a copy of this *Guide*.

Having the PDF file enables you to provide your students with each lesson's set of work sheets as you go, either as printed handouts or as individual PDFs for them to use on their pads, smartphones, etc. To obtain the PDF, go to www.thegogiver.com/tgworksheets.

Supplemental Material

The 2015 "expanded" edition of *The Go-Giver* provides some supplemental material, including a foreword, an authors' introduction, a discussion guide, and a Q&A with the authors. The foreword and introduction are treated here as part of the text and are covered in the final lesson of this curriculum. A few of the discussion guide's seventeen discussion questions have been incorporated into this curriculum, but the balance, as well as all fourteen pages of Q&A, are not. The educator may want to draw upon these for additional writing/discussion questions during the course.

The authors' companion volume, *Go-Givers Sell More*, can also provide the educator with additional reading and perspective on the topics of *The Go-Giver*; it is divided into five sections, each a collection of brief discourses on one of the Five Laws of Stratospheric Success.

Class Scheduling

Educators teach within a wide range of different schedule structures and requirements; clearly a "one size fits all" recipe for how to structure this curriculum would be hopelessly impractical. Randy Stelter likes teaching *The Go-Giver* over a two-week period of daily classes, covering one lesson every day or two. But he has also taught it over a two-month period. You will have your own circumstances to adapt to.

Since each lesson falls naturally into two halves, pre- and post- that lesson's assigned reading, the seven lessons could easily be taught as fourteen classes (perhaps with a fifteenth added at the end for discussing final projects). Or, for a more condensed course, you might combine the second (post-reading) half of each lesson with the first (pre-reading) half of the next.

Adapting This Curriculum for Other Age Groups

Educators using *The Go-Giver* in their coursework at undergraduate and graduate levels tell us they tend less to use the specific session-to-session structure in this *Guide* and focus more on in-class discussion of the book and its implications, and on in-depth projects (such as the dozen examples given in the Final Projects on pp. 61–62).

In these classes there is also typically more discussion and exploration of how the book's principles and ideas apply in the context of contemporary business. While nominally intended for the sales professional, the companion volume *Go-Givers Sell More* could also provide useful course material here.

We are not aware at this point of any teachers using the book with preteen students, but we have had correspondence from some fine young men and women of junior high and middle school age who have read the book and readily grasped its message. We would be delighted to correspond with anyone wishing to adapt this *Teacher's Guide* for use with younger students!

The Five Laws of Stratospheric Success

The Law of Value

*Your true worth is determined by
how much more you give in value than you take in payment.*

The Law of Compensation

*Your income is determined by
how many people you serve and how well you serve them.*

The Law of Influence

*Your influence is determined by
how abundantly you place other people's interests first.*

The Law of Authenticity

The most valuable gift you have to offer is yourself.

The Law of Receptivity

The key to effective giving is to stay open to receiving.

Excerpted with permission from *The Go-Giver: A Little Story About a Powerful Business Idea,* by Bob Burg and John David Mann (Portfolio/Penguin)

Lesson One
Chapters 1–2

Core Concept Discussion

What is *success*?

"Success" can mean different things to different people. When you hear the phrase, "a very successful person," what comes to mind for you?

How would you define success? Financially? Spiritually? Mentally? Physically? Relationally? Socially?

How would you consider yourself as successful?

What do you think it takes to be, or to become, a genuinely successful person?

Have you ever wished you could ask a highly successful person the keys to his or her success? What questions would you ask them?

Quick Write and Group Discussion

Write down the name of a person you consider to be highly successful. This can be someone from history, or someone alive today.

In the next two minutes, write down as many questions as you can think of that you would like to ask this person about how they became successful.

(After two minutes)

Put down your pen, form yourselves into groups of three, and share in your groups what you have written.

(After two or three minutes)

While still in your groups, take three minutes to consider this question: "What can you learn from successful people, and how can they influence you today?"

(After three minutes)

Now have one student from each of your groups report to the whole class what you discussed.

The Go-Giver's Laws of Success

In this course you will be reading a book about a man named Joe who learns many valuable business lessons, which also serve as life lessons. He learns these lessons primarily from a man named Pindar, but also from a number of Pindar's friends.

As you follow along with Joe on his journey, you will also learn about five key principles called the "Five Laws of Stratospheric Success." Joe will be asked to test out these each one of these five laws by applying it in his own life, immediately, the same day he learns it.

As you read we'll ask you to brainstorm ways you can apply these five laws in your own lives, too, just as Joe does.

Introduce Word Lists

Before each assigned reading, we'll hand out a word list to help learn the vocabulary for that reading.

Distribute the word list for Lesson One (paper copy or PDF) and engage students in activities to help learn these words.

Introduce Character Guides

The Go-Giver is a *parable*. A parable is a simple story told to make a point or teach a specific lesson.

A parable is fiction, but it's not the same thing as a novel. One major difference is that parables don't give a lot of detail about their characters. In fact, they intentionally keep things simple. For example, we never learn Joe's last name, or the name of the city or state where the story takes place.

Just because they're simple, though, doesn't mean there's not more going on than is obvious at first. As you read, we'll ask you to dig into the characters and see what you can learn about them.

The main character of this story is Joe—an "ordinary Joe." *The Go-Giver* traces the story of what happens to Joe and, more importantly, how Joe changes, over the course of one week. Every time Joe learns something new from Pindar or one of his friends, ask yourself, how do you think Joe will handle that lesson? Do you think it will lead him to do anything differently, and if so, how?

Distribute character guide for Lesson One (paper or PDF).

Each lesson's character guide will ask you to consider five questions for each new character you encounter:

1) What relationship does this character have to Joe?
2) What does this character want?
3) What does Joe learn from this character?
4) What have I learned from this character?
5) How can I model these lessons in my own life?

Assigned Reading
Chapters 1–2

Review
Review vocabulary and characters introduced so far.

Questions for Comprehension
For quiz and/or discussion

CHAPTER 1: THE GO-GETTER
1) As the story begins, Joe has a problem. That problem, and Joe's efforts to solve it, are what set the story in motion. What is that problem?
2) What two things does Joe feel he needs in order to land a large account?
3) What does Joe do to try and acquire these two things?
4) Who is Gus?
5) What are Joe's observations of Gus? Do you think they are accurate?

CHAPTER 2: THE SECRET
1) Who is "the Chairman"? Describe this character in detail.
2) What kind of voice does Pindar have?
3) According to Pindar, how often do successful people share their secrets?
4) Finish this statement: "Appearances can be _____. In fact, _____."
5) According to Pindar, in order to achieve stratospheric success, what do you need to have?
6) What is the Chairman's Trade Secret to success?
7) Pindar says, "Trying to be successful with making money as your goal is like trying to travel a superhighway at seventy miles an hour with your eyes glued to the rearview mirror." What do you think he means by that?
8) Finish this statement: "What you focus on is what you _____."
9) Finish this statement: "Ultimately, the world treats you more or less the way _____."

10) What image does Joe come up with to explain what keeps givers from being taken advantage of?
11) When must Joe apply each law?
12) Pindar says, "Most of us have grown up seeing the world as a place of limitation rather than as a place of inexhaustible treasures." What does this mean?
13) What is the "condition" Pindar places on Joe? What happens if Joe fails to meet that condition?
14) What is Pindar's "honor system"?
15) Why do you think this chapter is called "The Secret"? What is the secret that title refers to?

Going Deeper: Questions for Critical Thinking

WRITING EXERCISE
Why do you think a parable like this intentionally keeps things simple and doesn't add a lot of details about the characters' lives? How does that serve the story's purpose? How does that affect the reader's relationship to the story?

WRITING EXERCISE
In a paragraph, describe your reactions to and opinions of Joe and Pindar. What makes these two individuals respond the way they do?

WRITING EXERCISE
Joe is surprised at how easily he gets in to see Pindar, and further surprised when Pindar remarks on how often successful people are willing to share their "secrets" with others. How would you go about meeting someone you'd want to learn from?

WRITING EXERCISE
Pindar tells Joe, "The world treats you more or less the way you expect to be treated.... In fact, you'd be amazed at just how much *you* have to do with what happens *to* you." Do you agree? Why? or why not? Can you think of examples of how this may be true?

Word List*

Chapter 1
broker (2)
clout (2)
leverage (2)
underbid (2)
consultant (3)
eccentric (4)
pensioner (4)
relic (4)
erratic (4)
meerschaum (5)
Trade Secret (6)
crestfallen (6)

Chapter 2
enterprise (7)
mentoring (7)
stratospheric (8)
terrace (8)
bewilderment (11)
mindset (11)
parse (12)
ingenuity (13)
empathy (13)
exquisite (14)
non-disclosure agreements (NDA) (15)
abide (16)

*) Page numbers in all the Word Lists refer to the 2015 "Expanded Edition" of *The Go-Giver*.

Character Guide: Joe

Who is Joe?
_____
_____
_____
_____
_____

What does Joe want?
_____
_____
_____
_____
_____

What does Joe learn?
_____
_____
_____
_____
_____

What have I learned from Joe?
_____
_____
_____
_____
_____

How can I model these lessons in my own life?
_____
_____
_____
_____
_____

Character Guide: Carl Kellerman

What relationship does Carl have to Joe?

What does Carl want?

What does Joe learn from him?

What have I learned from him?

How can I model these lessons in my own life?

Character Guide: Pindar (the Chairman)

What relationship does Pindar have to Joe?

_____
_____
_____
_____
_____

What does Pindar want?

_____
_____
_____
_____
_____

What does Joe learn from him?

_____
_____
_____
_____
_____

What have I learned from him?

_____
_____
_____
_____
_____

How can I model these lessons in my own life?

_____
_____
_____
_____
_____

Character Guide: Gus

What relationship does Gus have to Joe?

___

What does Gus want?

___

What does Joe learn from him?

___

What have I learned from him?

___

How can I model these lessons in my own life?

Lesson Two
Chapters 3–4

Core Concept Discussion

What is *value*?

What does it mean when you say something "has value"?

The word "valuable" can describe so many different things, from valuables you keep in a safe (rare coins, jewelry, etc.), to valuable information, to a valuable experience or relationship. What defines something as "valuable"?

The authors define *giving* as "putting others' interests first and continually adding value to their lives." How many ways can you think of to "add value" to the lives of people you know?

Quick Write and Group Discussion

We also use the word "values" to describe those qualities or principles that we personally hold as most important, such as *integrity*, *adventure*, *family*, *loyalty*, *curiosity*, etcetera.

In the next two minutes, make a list of your own values, using single words to describe whatever different values are important to you.

(After two minutes)

What three words would you put at the top of that list? Take the next minute to look over your list and mark your top three choices with the numbers 1, 2, and 3. If you think of a new value you want to add, that's fine, too.

(After another minute)

Form yourselves into groups of three, and share in your groups what you've written.

(After two or three minutes)

Now have one student from each group report to the whole class what you discussed.

Preparation
Distribute word list and engage students in vocabulary activities (paper or PDF).
Distribute character guide (paper or PDF).
Distribute Five Laws journal for the Law of Value (paper or PDF).

Assigned Reading
Chapters 3–4

Review
Review vocabulary and characters introduced so far.

Questions for Comprehension
For quiz and/or discussion

CHAPTER 3: THE LAW OF VALUE
1) Who is the real estate magnate?
2) Were you surprised when you learned the identity of the real estate magnate?
3) Who did Pindar run into on his way to pick up his date?
4) How did Ernesto get started?
5) What does he own today?
6) How did his little hot dog stand grow into such a large business?
7) Finish this statement: "People will do business with and refer business to those people _____ _____."
8) What makes a great restaurant great? Is it the food?
9) What does Ernesto say about the question, "Does it make money"?
10) Finish this statement: "'Does it make money?' is not a bad question. It's a *great* question. It's just _____."
11) Why is this? What happens if you make "Does it make money?" the *first* question?
12) According to Pindar, how were all the fortunes of the world created?
13) What is the Golden Rule of Business?
14) Do you think this might be a valuable rule to adopt for yourself, when you begin doing business in the world? Why? Or if not, why not?
15) What is the Law of Value?

CHAPTER 4: THE CONDITION
1) What is the bad news Joe gets in this chapter?
2) What does Joe keep in his bottom drawer?
3) How does Joe apply Pindar's "condition" and put the Law of Value into practice?
4) What impact do you think that might have on Joe's situation, if any?

Going Deeper: Questions for Critical Thinking

WRITING EXERCISE

"It never hurts to be kind to people," says Pindar. Relate his story to a story of your own, a time when you were kind to someone whom you did not know. What happened?

WRITING EXERCISE

Joe mutters to himself, "This guy blows me off—and I give him a *referral*? And throw some good business at a *competitor*?!" Gus overhears him. What is Gus's response? In a paragraph, summarize why you think Gus reacted this way.

WRITING EXERCISE

The Law of Value says, "Your true worth is determined by how much more you give in value than you take in payment." You are a high school student who babysits or mows the neighbors' lawns. Explain how you might apply this first law right away, much as Joe is required to do.

WRITING EXERCISE

Ernesto explains what makes a bad restaurant, a good restaurant, and a great restaurant. What businesses do you know of that fit Ernesto's definition of greatness? How do they do it?

Five Laws Journal Discussion

Share with the class how you have applied the Law of Value in your own life.

Word List

Chapter 3

magnate (19)

résumé (19)

radiates (19)

gracious (20)

mortified (20)

stammered (22)

swanky (22)

marionette (22)

reputation (24)

persona (24)

riveting (24)

clientele (26)

grappled (38)

bona fide (29)

CEO (29)

Chapter 4

solitary (33)

pondered (33)

quota (33)

renewal (34)

referral (35)

Character Guide: Ernesto Iafrate

What relationship does Ernesto have to Joe?
_____
_____
_____
_____
_____

What does Ernesto want?
_____
_____
_____
_____
_____

What does Joe learn from him?
_____
_____
_____
_____
_____

What have I learned from him?
_____
_____
_____
_____
_____

How can I model these lessons in my own life?
_____
_____
_____
_____
_____

Character Guide: Jim Galloway

What relationship does Jim have to Joe?
_____
_____
_____
_____
_____

What does Jim want?
_____
_____
_____
_____
_____

What does Joe learn from him?
_____
_____
_____
_____
_____

What have I learned from him?
_____
_____
_____
_____
_____

How can I model these lessons in my own life?
_____
_____
_____
_____
_____

Character Guide: Ed Barnes

What relationship does Ed have to Joe?

What does Ed want?

What does Joe learn from him?

What have I learned from him?

How can I model these lessons in my own life?

Five Laws Journal

The Law of Value says:
_____
_____
_____

How did I apply this law today?

DATE   DESCRIPTION

Lesson Three
Chapters 5–7

Core Concept Discussion

What is *service*?

"Service" has so many different meanings. It can mean being in the military; serving someone a meal; a religious ceremony; helping out at a community soup kitchen; or how you treat a customer at work. What do all these things have in common?

What does it mean to *serve* someone else?

In chapter 5 you'll read about a character who says, "If you want to have more success, serve more people." In the same chapter, this character also quotes Martin Luther King, Jr., saying: "Anyone can be great, because everybody can serve." What does serving have to do with being *great* or *successful*?

Quick Write and Group Discussion

Write down the names of three people you consider as *great*, *highly successful*, or both.

In the next two minutes, under each name write down how exactly you think each person *serves* or *served* others.

(After two minutes)

Form yourselves into groups of three, and share in your groups what you've written.

(After two or three minutes)

Now have one student from each group report to the whole class what you discussed.

Preparation
Distribute word list and engage students in vocabulary activities.
Distribute character guide.
Distribute Five Laws journal for the Law of Compensation.

Assigned Reading
Chapters 5–7

Review
Review vocabulary and characters introduced so far.

Questions for Comprehension
For quiz and/or discussion

CHAPTER 5: THE LAW OF COMPENSATION
1) Who is the CEO in this chapter?
2) Were you surprised when you learned the identity of the CEO?
3) Describe the scene in the first conference room Joe enters at Learning Systems for Children. How does Joe react when he sees it?
4) How did LSC start?
5) What is the Law of Compensation?
6) Nicole Martin says, "Your compensation is directly proportional to how many lives you touch." Do you agree with this statement? What is Joe's reaction to Nicole's observation?
7) Joe observes that people's compensation is not simply a reflection of their *value*, but of something else. What is that something else?
8) Finish this statement of Nicole's: "If you want more success, find a way to _____." What do you think about that statement?
9) Why did Nicole nearly sabotage her business? Do you think this happens in real life?
10) Finish this statement of Nicole's: "Being broke and being rich are both _____." What do you think about this statement?
11) Are there limitations to what you can earn? Why, or why not?
12) This chapter is the second time Joe has heard about this character called simply "the Connector." As you continue reading, try to predict who this person might be.

CHAPTER 6: SERVING COFFEE
1) How does Joe apply the Law of Compensation?
2) What impact do you think that might have, if any?
3) Gus asks Joe, "How did it feel to serve all those people?" What is Joe's response?
4) Complete this statement of Gus's: "Sometimes you feel foolish, but you _____ _____."
5) Why do you think the authors titled this chapter "Serving Coffee"? (Remember this question; you my find it has deeper implications later on.)

CHAPTER 7: RACHEL
1) At what age did Rachel start working?

2) What jobs did she do?
3) How did she approach each one?
4) What are the three universal reasons for working?
5) Of these three, which one do most people focus on? Which one do genuinely successful people focus on?
6) The last paragraph of this chapter is an example of *foreshadowing*. What is foreshadowing, and why do you think writers use this technique?
7) Joe senses that there is more to Rachel's story. If you had to guess, where do you think her story could possibly lead?

Going Deeper: Questions for Critical Thinking

WRITING EXERCISE

In a paragraph, discuss some ways you can find to serve more people—in your community, your school, your place of worship, your family, etc.

WRITING EXERCISE

Nicole says she used to believe that there are two types of people in the world: those who get rich and those who do good. Do you see a basic contradiction between being a good person and being a wealthy person—or to put it another way, between giving and receiving?

WRITING EXERCISE

Hiding the CEO's identity at first and then making it a surprise is a narrative device called a *reveal* (sometimes called "plot twist"). Why do you think the authors use this technique in *The Go-Giver*? Similar little mysteries/reveals are planted throughout the story. As you read, start a running list and see how many you can identify.

WRITING EXERCISE

When Joe says he felt "like an idiot" when he served coffee to everyone on his floor, Gus comments, "*Sometimes you feel foolish, even look foolish, but you do the thing anyway.*" Have there been times when you felt foolish but did the thing anyway, and which ultimately lead to great reward?

Five Laws Journal Discussion

Share with the class how you have applied the Law of Compensation in your own life.

Word List

Chapter 5

proffered (37)

inadvertent (37)

teleconferencing (37)

delirious (38)

unbridled (38)

exuberance (38)

Yorick (38)

gaped (38)

constrained (41)

fledgling (42)

proportional (43)

marshal (43)

arbitrary (43)

exultant (43)

pensive (44)

rueful (44)

Chapter 6

vaguely (50)

tweed (51)

Chapter 7

anxious (54)

invariably (54)

diverse (55)

undeniable (56)

Character Guide: Nicole Martin

What relationship does Nicole have to Joe?

What does Nicole want?

What does Joe learn from her?

What have I learned from her?

How can I model these lessons in my own life?

Character Guide: Rachel

What relationship does Rachel have to Joe?

_____
_____
_____
_____
_____

What does Rachel want?

_____
_____
_____
_____
_____

What does Joe learn from her?

_____
_____
_____
_____
_____

What have I learned from her?

_____
_____
_____
_____
_____

How can I model these lessons in my own life?

_____
_____
_____
_____
_____

Five Laws Journal

The Law of Compensation says:
_____
_____
_____

How did I apply this law today?
   DATE   DESCRIPTION
_____
_____
_____
_____
_____
_____
_____
_____
_____
_____
_____
_____
_____
_____
_____
_____
_____
_____
_____
_____
_____
_____

Lesson Four
Chapters 8–9

Core Concept Discussion

What is *influence*?

What does it mean to *influence* or to *have influence on* another person?

In any group, from a class or club to an entire society, certain people tend to have more influence than others, or to influence greater numbers of people. Why do you think that is? What is it that makes some people especially influential?

Quick Write and Group Discussion

Write down the name of a person who has been a strong influence in making you who you are today.

In the next two minutes, write down what it is about that person that has made him or her so influential in your life.

(After two minutes)

Form yourselves into groups of three, and share in your groups what you've written.

(After two or three minutes)

Now have one student from each group report to the whole class what you discussed.

Preparation
Distribute Word List and engage students in vocabulary activities.
Distribute Character Guide.
Distribute Five Laws Journal for the Law of Influence.

Assigned Reading
Chapters 8–9

Review
Review vocabulary and characters introduced so far.

Questions for Comprehension
For quiz and/or discussion

CHAPTER 8: THE LAW OF INFLUENCE
1) What occupies the twenty-fourth floor of the Liberty Life Insurance and Financial Services Company?
2) Sam Rosen accounts for more than three-quarters of what?
3) What was Sam's first job?
4) According to Sam, one of the keys to his success was developing his *network*. How does he define a "network"?
5) Finish this sentence: "They're people who are personally invested in _____."
6) Why, according to Sam, are those people personally invested in that?
7) What is an "army of personal walking ambassadors"?
8) What does Sam mean when he says, "Stop keeping score"?
9) Finish this statement: "Fifty-fifty's a losing proposition. The only winning proposition is _____."
10) What does Pindar describe as "enlightened self-interest"?
11) What, according to Pindar, is the one thing that Ernesto, Nicole, and Sam all have in common?
12) What is the Law of Influence?
13) Why, according to Pindar, does the Law of Influence work?

CHAPTER 9: SUSAN
1) What is going on at the office when Joe returns?
2) Most of this chapter takes place in Joe and Susan's home. Why do you think the authors chose this setting for Joe to start coming to the realizations he does?
3) What is the "unwritten rule" in Joe and Susan's marriage?
4) Do you think this a good rule for your significant relationships? Why, or why not?
5) In the middle of talking with Susan, what does Joe suddenly remember about his conversation with Sam?
6) How does this shift what Joe says and does? What is Susan's response?
7) How does Joe apply the Law of Influence?
8) What impact does that have, if any?
9) What additional impact do you think it might have for Joe in the future, if any?

Going Deeper: Questions for Critical Thinking

WRITING EXERCISE

Write a list of ten people whom you would consider as members of your own *army of personal walking ambassadors*. Discuss in detail what it is you *know, like and trust* about each of these people. What characteristics about yourself do you think cause them to know, like and trust you? If you could change a few things about yourself, or if there are certain characteristics that you would like to more strongly develop in yourself, what would they be? How does one go about changing or strengthening one's own character?

WRITING EXERCISE

Sam tells Joe that what makes an influential person influential is not money, position, or accomplishments, but how abundantly they put others' interests ahead of their own. Do you agree? Who are the most influential people in your life? Do they fit this definition?

WRITING EXERCISE

What is the biggest thing you learned from chapter 9, "Susan"? In a paragraph, describe what impact you think that could have on your life, both now and in the future.

Five Laws Journal Discussion

Share with the class how you have applied the Law of Influence in your own life.

Word List

Chapter 8

filigree (59)	abundant (63)
policies (59)	enlightened (64)
sumptuous (60)	beatific (64)
negotiator (60)	magnetic (64)
mediator (60)	

Chapter 9

philanthropist (60)	chaos (69)
amassed (61)	listless (70)
network (61)	imposing (70)
invested (62)	wan (71)
ambassadors (62)	lurched (73)
creditor (63)	generosity (74)
proposition (63)	

Character Guide: Sam Rosen

What relationship does Sam have to Joe?

What does Sam want?

What does Joe learn from him?

What have I learned from him?

How can I model these lessons in my own life?

Character Guide: Susan

What relationship does Susan have to Joe?
_____
_____
_____
_____
_____

What does Susan want?
_____
_____
_____
_____
_____

What does Joe learn from her?
_____
_____
_____
_____
_____

What have I learned from her?
_____
_____
_____
_____
_____

How can I model these lessons in my own life?
_____
_____
_____
_____
_____

Five Laws Journal

The Law of Influence says:
_____
_____
_____

How did I apply this law today?

DATE   DESCRIPTION

Lesson Five
Chapters 10–11

Core Concept Discussion

What does it mean to be *authentic*?

How do you know when someone is being authentic or not?

What does it feel like when you are being authentic with someone, and what does it feel like when you are *not* being authentic?

What effect does being more authentic have on those around you? How does it make others feel?

What is the difference between authenticity and saying or doing whatever you feel like, whenever you feel like it? When is it not appropriate to be 100 percent transparent?

Quick Write and Group Discussion

Write down two names: 1) someone famous who seems to you an especially good example of authenticity, and 2) someone you know personally who is also a good example of authenticity.

In the next two minutes, under both names write down as many examples as you can of when and how these two people struck you as authentic, including what they said or did.

(After two minutes)

Form yourselves into groups of three, and share in your groups what you've written.

(After two or three minutes)

Now have one student from each group report to the whole class what you discussed.

Preparation
Distribute word list and engage students in vocabulary activities.
Distribute character guide.
Distribute Five Laws journal for the Law of Authenticity.

Assigned Reading
Chapters 10–11

Review

Review vocabulary and characters introduced so far.

Questions for Comprehension
For quiz and/or discussion

CHAPTER 10: THE LAW OF AUTHENTICITY

1) In chapter 10, what does Pindar do for the first time regarding his "condition"?
2) What does Pindar mean by "improving your life's balance sheet"?
3) Why does Pindar believe his marriage has lasted so long?
4) What were the three gifts Debra Davenport got on her forty-second birthday?
5) Why does she describe her husband's walking out on her, obviously a painful experience, as a "gift"?
6) What does she mean when she says it took her a full year "to unwrap, open, understand, and use" that gift?
7) What gift did she get a year later, for her forty-*third* birthday?
8) What question did she ask at the symposium? What was the answer?
9) What did Debra do differently on the house she sold when she was about to quit?
10) What did Debra know how to do after years of being "a mom, wife and household manager"?
11) What, according to Debra, is the most valuable thing you can give?
12) What is the Law of Authenticity?
13) What does Debra Davenport's story have to do with the Law of Authenticity?
14) Why does Joe say he first came to see Pindar, and why does he say it?
15) What does Pindar say about that?

CHAPTER 11: GUS

1) Gus suspects that Joe is experiencing "the cleansing pain of honest self-reflection." Is that true? If so, how so? What does that phrase mean?
2) Who is "the Connector"?
3) Were you surprised to learn the Connector's identity?
4) What do we learn about Gus and his career in this chapter?
5) What is it that Gus shares with Joe that is so private, he wants it to remain confidential?
6) When the story says, "Gus named a figure," why do you think the authors don't tell us what that figure is?
7) Why does Gus work at the Clason-Hill Trust Corporation?
8) How does Joe apply the Law of Authenticity?
9) What impact do you think this has, if any?

10) Who do you think the Friday Guest, whom Joe is supposed to meet on Friday at Pindar's home, might be?

Going Deeper: Questions for Critical Thinking

WRITING EXERCISE

Joe observes more than once how effectively Debra Davenport connects with her audience. Going back through her speech, how many specific moments can you identify when she does this? Make list of all these moments, and then explain, in each case, exactly how or why you think that happens.

WRITING EXERCISE

Have you ever had an experience like Debra Davenport's, when you stopped trying to be someone you weren't and just let yourself be yourself—and had a surprisingly good outcome happen? In a paragraph, describe that experience, including both what happened and what it felt like.

WRITING EXERCISE

What stops people from being authentic? What is the connection between being authentic and being vulnerable? What is the connection between being authentic and being powerful? In a paragraph, answer these three questions using examples from your own personal experience.

Five Laws Journal Discussion

Share with the class how you have applied the Law of Authenticity in your own life.

Word List

Chapter 10

aria (77)

woes (77)

query (77)

symposium (79)

high-water mark (79)

methodology (81)

concession (81)

deadpanned (81)

riff (82)

assumptive (82)

kill clause (82)

leveraged asset (82)

takeaway (82)

bravura (82)

mundane (83)

commodity (83)

liability (84)

exasperation (85)

impassive (88)

Sphinx (88)

inaudible (89)

Chapter 11

contrite (93)

ambled (96)

Character Guide: Debra Davenport

What relationship does Debra have to Joe?

_____

What does Debra want?

_____

What does Joe learn from her?

_____

What have I learned from her?

_____

How can I model these lessons in my own life?

_____

Five Laws Journal

The Law of Authenticity says:
_____
_____
_____

How did I apply this law today?

    DATE   DESCRIPTION

Lesson Six
Chapters 12–13

Core Concept Discussion

What is the connection between *giving* and *receiving*?

The first four Laws of Stratospheric Success all have to do with giving, in some way. The fifth law, which you'll read about in chapter 12, has to do with *receiving*. Why do you think, in a book about the power of giving, the authors would devote a whole chapter to receiving?

Have you ever heard the expression, "It is better to give than to receive"? What do you think about that?

Quick Write and Group Discussion

In the next minute, write down a list of the biggest, most important, and most valuable things you've ever received.

(After one minute)

Reviewing that list, how many of the things you've written were the result of someone else's giving?

In the next minute, write a list of the biggest, most important, and most valuable things you've ever given.

(After one minute)

Now, reviewing this second list: how were each of those gifts received?

Form yourselves into groups of three, and share in your groups what you've written.

(After two or three minutes)

Now have one student from each group report to the whole class what you discussed.

Preparation

Distribute word list and engage students in vocabulary activities.
Distribute character guide.
Distribute Five Laws journal for the Law of Receptivity.

Assigned Reading
Chapters 12–13

Review
Review vocabulary and characters introduced so far.

Questions for Comprehension
For quiz and/or discussion

CHAPTER 12: THE LAW OF RECEPTIVITY
1) What do we learn about Rachel's background in this chapter?
2) What has Rachel been doing for the past year?
3) When Pindar says *giving*, what's the first thing that comes to Joe's mind?
4) What is the "traditional wisdom nonsense" Pindar says was drummed into most of us when we were young?
5) How does Pindar illustrate the connection between giving and receiving?
6) What, according to Pindar, is the natural result of giving?
7) Complete this statement of Pindar's: "Inside every truth and appearance, there's a bit of _____." What examples can you think of that illustrate this observation?
8) What is the Law of Receptivity?
9) Who is the Friday guest?

CHAPTER 13: FULL CIRCLE
1) Why does Gus say, "You want to come in off that ledge and talk about it before you jump?"
2) Complete this statement of Gus's: "The point is not *what you do*. Not *what you accomplish*. It's _____." What do you think he means by this?
3) Gus offers to clean up while Joe goes home. How might things have worked out differently if Joe had taken him up on that offer?
4) Joe gets an unexpected phone call at six fifteen, long after their office would normally be closed. Who is the call from?
5) That call would not have come if Joe hadn't done something, much earlier in the story, that appeared insignificant at the time. What was that action?
6) Why do you think this chapter is titled "Full Circle"?
7) In the last line of the chapter, Joe says, "I just might know someone." Whom is he referring to?
8) How does Joe apply the Law of Receptivity? And what impact do you think this might have?

48

Going Deeper: Questions for Critical Thinking

WRITING EXERCISE

Paraphrase and explain in your own words the following quote from chapter 12: "The world certainly was designed with a sense of humor, wasn't it? Inside every truth and every appearance there's a bit of *opposite* tucked inside."

WRITING EXERCISE

In chapter 13, Gus tells Joe he is "a different person than you were a week ago." Do you think this is true, and if so, how? If you had to identify a single moment in the story when Joe makes this shift, what would it be?

WRITING EXERCISE

The phone call that happens at the end of chapter 13 is about to change Joe's life forever, in a powerfully positive way. But a number of critical factors had to come together to create that outcome, including: 1) one person whom Joe barely knows (Ed Barnes) referring him to another person whom Joe doesn't know at all (Neil Hansen); 2) Joe happening to know all about Rachel's expertise and network of connections in the coffee world; and 3) Joe being there in the office, more than an hour after quitting time and long after everyone else has left, to be the one who fields this call.

These all seem like coincidences; but are they really? Can you trace each factor back to its point of origin?

Have you ever had this sort of thing happen to you, "out of the blue," that turned out to be a strongly positive thing in your life? If so, describe it in a paragraph, and then answer the question: do you think it was a coincidence?

Five Laws Journal Discussion

Share with the class how you have applied the Law of Receptivity in your own life.

Word List

Chapter 12

- muted (97)
- entrepreneurs (98)
- consternation (100)
- vibrant (104)
- ravenous (104)
- grapple (104)
- irony (105)
- paradox (105)

Chapter 13

- somber (109)
- conjure (109)
- pragmatic (111)
- forlorn (111)
- dissipate (111)
- ebbing (112)
- illustrious (112)
- contentment (112)
- receptive (112)
- minnow (113)
- concession (114)

Character Guide: Neil Hansen

What relationship does Neil have to Joe?

_____
_____
_____
_____
_____

What does Neil want?

_____
_____
_____
_____
_____

What does Joe learn from him?

_____
_____
_____
_____
_____

What have I learned from him?

_____
_____
_____
_____
_____

How can I model these lessons in my own life?

_____
_____
_____
_____
_____

Five Laws Journal

The Law of Receptivity says:
_____
_____
_____

How did I apply this law today?

   DATE   DESCRIPTION

Lesson Seven
Chapter 14, Foreword, Introduction

Core Concept Discussion

What is *success*?

We started the class with the question, "What is success?" Now that we've nearly worked our way through the entire book, let's revisit that question.

Here is a sampling of how a number of famous people have answered that question.

(Hand out sheet: "Definitions of Success / More Reflections on Success")

What does success look like for you?

Quick Write and Group Discussion

Close your eyes for a moment, and imagine yourself, ten years from now, as extremely successful—not some other person, but an extremely successful version of *you*.

(After 20 or 30 seconds)

Now take the next two minutes to write out a description of what that extremely successful *you* looks like.

(After two minutes)

Form yourselves into groups of three, and share in your groups what you've written.

(After two or three minutes)

Now have one student from each group report to the whole class what you discussed.

Preparation
Distribute word list and engage students in vocabulary activities.
Distribute character guide.

Assigned Reading
Chapter 14, Foreword, and Introduction

Review
Review vocabulary and characters.

Questions for Comprehension
For quiz and/or discussion

CHAPTER 14: THE GO-GIVER
1) How much time has elapsed as chapter 14 opens? What can the reader infer about what Joe has accomplished in the meantime?
2) When a magazine article refers to "one of those sweetheart deals that comes along once in a lifetime, if then," what is it referring to?
3) Who are the three partners of the business Claire is visiting?
4) What is Claire's response when Joe thanks her for seeing him? Does that remind you of another scene earlier in the book?
5) How does Claire respond when Joe tells her she hasn't gotten the job she was applying for?
6) What *does* Joe hire Claire to do, and why?
7) Claire is clearly very interested in Joe's job offer, but she says there is something else she is even more interested in. What is that?
8) Claire asks Joe a question, but the chapter ends before Joe has a chance to answer it. Why do you think the authors ended it this way, without Joe giving her a full answer? How would *you* answer that question?
9) Who do you think Claire was going to meet?
10) How many times in the book do the authors actually use the term, "go-giver"?

FOREWORD
1) What does Ms. Huffington cover in her first sentence?
2) Complete this statement: "That's not just a children's fairy tale—it's a good description of _____."
3) What forces, according to Ms. Huffington, can pressure us into doubting whether the principles of *The Go-Giver* actually work in the real world?
4) How does the Foreword define what it means to "be a giver"?

INTRODUCTION
1) In the first paragraph the authors tell us about two men who decide to help a colleague whose business is on the brink of failure. What is the point of this brief story? and how does it relate to the central point of *The Go-Giver*?

2) According to the authors, not only companies and businesspeople but also "parents, teachers, pastors and counselors" have used the book in their work and their lives. Why might this be? Does this remind you of anything that Pindar told Joe about these principles?
3) Finish this statement: While the world may at times appear to be a dog-eat-dog place, there is actually _____."

Going Deeper: Questions for Critical Thinking

WRITING EXERCISE

Three of Pindar's friends—Ernesto, Nicole, and Sam—spell out the first three laws to Joe, directly and explicitly. The fourth law comes a little more indirectly as part of Debra Davenport's public talk. And nobody tells Joe what the fifth law is, or even what it's called. Why do you think the authors had Pindar set things up this way?

WRITING EXERCISE

When he meets Ernesto, Joe at first has no idea that he is one of Pindar's masters of stratospheric success. The same thing happens the following day with Nicole. Do you think the authors did this to make a deeper point? There are at least four other characters in the story whose full role eventually surprises Joe. Can you identify those four?

WRITING EXERCISE

Joe first visited the Chairman because he was hoping to get "some big guns" to win back the deal he just lost, and he believed Pindar would give him "clout and leverage." Does he end up getting what he went looking for? If so, how? And if not, why not?

WRITING EXERCISE

Who was the most interesting person in the book for you? Whom did you most identify with throughout the book? What did this person teach you that you can apply in your life?

Five Laws Journal Discussion

Discuss what new ways you've found to apply all Five Laws of Stratospheric Success in your own life.

WRITING EXERCISE & GROUP DISCUSSION

Of the Five Laws, which was the easiest for you to put into practice? Why? Which was the most difficult or challenging? Why?

Definitions of Success

"Success is ...

"The progressive realization of a worthy goal." — Earl Nightingale

"To be able to spend your life in your own way." — Christopher Morley

"Liking yourself, liking what you do, and liking how you do it." — Maya Angelou

"Having the courage, the determination, and the will to become the person you believe you were meant to be." — George Sheehan

"Peace of mind, that is the direct result of knowing that you have done your best, at becoming the best you are capable of becoming." — Coach John Wooden

"Doing ordinary things extraordinarily well." — Jim Rohn

"The sum of small efforts, repeated day-in and day-out." — Robert Collier

"Stumbling from failure to failure with no loss of enthusiasm." — Winston Churchill

"Measured not so much by the position that one has reached in life as by the obstacles which he has overcome while trying to succeed." — Booker T. Washington

"Inner peace. That's a good day for me." — Denzel Washington

"To laugh often and much, to win the respect of intelligent people and the affection of children, to earn the appreciation of honest critics and endure the betrayal of false friends, to appreciate beauty, to find the best in others, to leave the world a bit better, whether by a healthy child, a garden patch, or a redeemed social condition; to know even one life has breathed easier because you have lived." — Ralph Waldo Emerson

More Reflections on Success

"Don't aim at success—the more you aim at it and make it a target, the more you are going to miss it. For success, like happiness, cannot be pursued; it must *ensue*, and it only does so as the unintended side-effect of one's dedication to a cause greater then oneself." — Viktor E. Frankl, in *Man's Search for Meaning*

"Definiteness of purpose is the starting point of all achievement." — W. Clement Stone

"The more you're actively and practically engaged, the more successful you will feel." — Richard Branson

"Successful and unsuccessful people do not vary greatly in their abilities. They vary in their desires to reach their potential." — John Maxwell

"Would you like me to give you a formula for success? It's quite simple, really. Double your rate of failure. You are thinking of failure as the enemy of success. But it isn't at all. You can be discouraged by failure or you can learn from it. So go ahead and make mistakes. Make all you can. Because remember that's where you will find success." — Thomas Watson

"Success does not consist in never making mistakes but in never making the same one a second time." — George Bernard Shaw

"I attribute my success to this: I never gave or took any excuse." — Florence Nightingale

"Don't let the noise of others' opinions drown out your own inner voice. And most important, have the courage to follow your heart and intuition. They somehow already know what you truly want to become. Everything else is secondary." — Steve Jobs

"A successful man is one who can lay a firm foundation with the bricks others have thrown at him." — David Brinkley

"Let no feeling of discouragement prey upon you, and in the end you are sure to succeed." — Abraham Lincoln

"Twenty years from now you will be more disappointed by the things that you didn't do than by the ones you did do, so throw off the bowlines, sail away from safe harbor, catch the trade winds in your sails. Explore, dream, discover." — Mark Twain

Word List

Chapter 14

catapult (117)
boutique (118)
quaint (118)
tiered (119)
freelancer (120)
indigenous (121)
indigenous (125)

Foreword

cynicism (xiii)
resignation (xiii)
quid pro quo (xiv)

Introduction

peer group (xv)
closure (xv)
brink (xv)
Chambers of Commerce (xv)
precepts (xv)
matrimonial (xvi)
counterintuitive (xvi)
expat (xvi)
compatriot (xvi)
turnaround (xvii)
implement (xvii)

Character Guide: Claire

What relationship does Claire have to Joe?

_____
_____
_____
_____
_____

What does Claire want?

_____
_____
_____
_____
_____

What does Joe learn from her?

_____
_____
_____
_____
_____

What have I learned from her?

_____
_____
_____
_____
_____

How can I model these lessons in my own life?

_____
_____
_____
_____
_____

Final Projects

We *recommend assigning your students a final project toward the end of the session, to give them an opportunity to further deepen their understanding of the book and to ground its lessons in their own experience. Here are just a dozen examples; the possibilities are infinite!*

1) PROFILE A FAMOUS GO-GIVER
Research a famous person (historical or present-day) whom you consider genuinely successful, and find out what drove them to become the person they did. What was their vision? How did they make it happen? What value did they provide to others? How did they manage to touch many lives with their talents? How did any of the Five Laws play a role in their success?

2) PROFILE A "GREAT" GO-GIVER BUSINESS
Find a present-day example of a "great business," using Ernesto Iafrate's definition, whose history closely parallels Ernesto's—humble beginnings, a flourishing reputation, eventual stratospheric growth and success. Write a profile of that business, including as many examples as you can of how its history and operation echoes Iafrate's.

3) PRESENT THE FIVE LAWS PERSONIFIED
Create a multimedia essay that profiles five different well-known personalities, each one chosen to illustrate a different one of the Five Laws of Stratospheric Success. Include explanations as to why each one exemplifies that law, along with specific examples from your subjects' lives and careers. Your essay should include images, sound, and text (video clips optional).

4) CREATE YOUR OWN STORIES
Collaborating with a partner or small group, create your own Go-Giver stories using examples from your own lives that illustrate all five of the Five Laws of Stratospheric Success. Make sure to have your stories illustrate specifically how you have applied these laws in your everyday lives, and how doing this has affected you and those around you.

5) SELL A MOVIE IDEA
Collaborating with a partner or small group, write a proposal for selling the idea of producing a movie from *The Go-Giver* to a Hollywood production company. Your proposal should include a list of current actors and actresses who should play each character in the book, and a complete script for one full scene from the movie, complete with dialogue and scene directions.

6) FILL IN THE MISSING EVENTS

Write a paper describing in detail what you imagine happens to the characters in *The Go-Giver* during the ten months that elapse between the end of chapter 13 and the beginning of chapter 14, including Joe, Susan, Rachel, Neil Hansen, and as many other characters from the story as you can. Do you think it was all smooth sailing? Or if any problems or challenges cropped up, what were they, and how did the characters deal with them?

7) CREATE AN ADAPTATION FOR FIRST GRADERS

Reframe the story of *The Go-Giver*, making the main characters young children (ages 6 to 9) and putting Joe in a situation appropriate to a child. Write out your adapted story in summary form, and rephrase the Five Laws using language that a six-year-old could easily grasp and understand.

8) DESIGN A GO-GIVER CURRICULUM FOR MIDDLE SCHOOLERS

Design an educational curriculum for middle schoolers (ages ten to thirteen) including a complete set of lessons and perspectives for all Five Laws of Stratospheric Success. Discuss the unique issues that preteens face today and how as a teacher you would use this curriculum to guide them.

9) CONSULT TO A BUSINESS

Imagine you are business consultant, like Pindar. A large company has hired you to help improve their sales and profitability. Write a paper describing this business and their current situation, followed by the recommendations you come up with for them. Make sure your recommendations utilize all five of the Five Laws of Stratospheric Success, and in your paper explain how each recommendation uses the Laws and how it will help that business.

10) CREATE A GO-GIVER COMMUNITY PROJECT

Create and implement a community project that helps people in your community using all five of the Laws of Stratospheric Success. After several weeks of implementing your project, write a report on how it is working and what you are learning from it.

11) CREATE A GO-GIVER PROGRAM TO STOP BULLYING

Bullying is a problem in schools nationwide. Create and implement a project that uses the principles of *The Go-Giver* to address bullying in your own school community, both to halt bullying and to advocate for the victims of bullying. Write a report on your program, including both a description of the program itself and of what impact you see it having.

12) DEVELOP A GO-GIVER PROBLEM-SOLVING STRATEGY

Choose a problem that affects students on your campus. Describe the problem and the impact it has on students and the community. Utilizing the principles of *The Go-Giver*, develop a program that proactively addresses the problem. Consider using education, team-building, and buddy systems to actively engage students in participating and learning.

Resources

Work Sheets PDF
A PDF file including the complete set of work sheets for the *Teacher's Guide* can be downloaded at: www.thegogiver.com/tgworksheets.

Further Reading
Additional books in the Go-Giver series:
Go-Givers Sell More, Bob Burg and John David Mann (2010)
The Go-Giver Leader, Bob Burg and John David Mann (2016)

Other parables:
The One Minute Manager, Ken Blanchard and Spencer Johnson, M.D. (1982)
The Richest Man in Babylon, George S. Clason (1926)
The Alchemist, Paul Coelho (1988)
The Greatest Salesman in the World, Og Mandino (1968)
The Little Prince, Antoine de Sainte-Exupéry (1943)

Websites
www.thegogiver.com – *the book's official website*
www.gogiverspeaker.com – *offers a certification program to become a Go-Giver speaker*
www.burg.com – *coauthor's website and blog*
www.johndavidmann.com – *coauthor's website and blog*

Bulk Purchases
Copies of *The Go-Giver* may be purchased at bulk discounts from these resellers:

800-CEO-READ
www.800ceoread.com
Aaron Schleicher, Author Services: 800-236-7323 ext. 204 or (414) 220-4459

BookPal
www.book-pal.com
Meghan Falk: 866-522-6657 ext. 245 or (949) 205-7212

Thanks

We don't really know much about Ed Barnes, or Jim Galloway, or even Neil Hansen. But we do know this: without all three of them, Joe would never have been able to create Rachel's Famous Coffee, and his story would have ended with a whimper instead of a bang.

The same is true for this *Teacher's Guide* project: there are so many Jim Galloways to thank!

First in line is Randy's good friend and most excellent boss, Don Gandy, principal of Wheeler High School in Valparaiso, Indiana. Without Don's support and passion for their resource reading program and for implementing the Go-Giver books in the school, this *Guide* would likely not exist. (Randy is not the only one who teaches the Go-Giver books at Wheeler!)

Next in line are all those people who have in one way or another added weight to this wisp of an idea and helped to move it forward, including Casey Cornelius, Aimee Costello, David Fuehrer, Sonny Lubick, Andy Mack, Chris Mack, Angela Maiers, Owen McCarthy, Jacquie Mozrall, Connie Nolen, Tim Peterson, Nido Qubein, Melinda Rangel, Bill Shuster, Jennifer Smetana, Pat Sullivan, Stephanie Widner, Christie Whitbeck, Kelli Winarski, Julie Woods, Yolanda Young, and dozens of others. Don and Randy lit the match and started the fire going—and soon this steady parade of people began stopping by and adding on new kindling and logs, until this thing had built into a blaze that told us it was time to take action and *put it into publication.*

That fire would have never taken hold if it weren't for the invaluable input and tireless effort of three people who collaborated and supported at every turn: Maureen Stelter, who has spent countless hours in reviewing, revising, and helping to shape this *Guide* into what it could become; Kathy Tagenel, who is the creative and operational heart of Go-Givers International; and Ana Gabriel Mann, a former professor and lifelong educator, who has championed this project and the idea of teaching *The Go-Giver* in schools at every turn.

Then there are those who helped us set up the fireplace and hearth in the first place, including our always amazing team at Portfolio and our stratospherically great literary agents, Margret McBride and Faye Atchison.

And we saved the best for last: our thanks to *you*, dear reader, for using this *Guide*, for all the students whose lives you've touched and will touch, and for the difference you make in the world.

About the Authors

Randy Stelter is an English teacher and the athletic director at Wheeler High School in Valparaiso, Indiana. He has been teaching since 1979 and has been teaching *The Go-Giver* to his students since 2009. He was nominated by former students and selected to "Who's Who Among America's Teachers" seven times, and selected for the Charles F. Mass District I Indiana Athletic Administrator's Distinguished Service Award in 2008 by the Indiana High School Athletic Association and his peers. Randy has coached football, basketball and softball for over twenty-five years, coaching or administrating programs that have earned six State Championships as well as being named conference "Coach of the Year." He served on the *Chicago Sun-Times* and *Chicago Tribune's* All-State Committee for numerous years. He also created the class and wrote the curriculum guide for *English for Men*, a subject he taught for eight years.

Bob Burg is coauthor of the *Wall Street Journal* bestseller *The Go-Giver* and its companion volumes *Go-Givers Sell More* and *The Go-Giver Leader*. A former television personality and top-producing salesperson, Bob speaks to corporations, organizations, and at sales and leadership conferences worldwide on topics at the core of the *Go-Giver* books. Addressing audiences ranging from sixty to sixteen thousand, Bob has shared the platform with some of today's top business leaders, broadcast personalities, coaches, athletes, and political leaders, including a former U.S. president. He is also the author of *Adversaries into Allies* and the classic *Endless Referrals*, which has sold more than a quarter of a million copies and is still used today as a training manual in many corporations. He was named by the American Management Association as one of the Top 30 Most Influential Thought Leaders in Business for 2014.

John David Mann has been writing about business, leadership, and the laws of success for more than thirty years. As a high school student, he led a group of friends in creating their own successful high school. After establishing himself as a concert cellist and prizewinning composer, he built a multimillion-dollar sales organization of more than a hundred thousand people before turning to writing and publishing. In addition to coauthoring the *Go-Giver* books with Bob Burg, John is also coauthor of the *New York Times* bestsellers *Flash Foresight* (with Daniel Burrus) and *The Red Circle* (with Brandon Webb) and the national bestseller *Among Heroes* (with Brandon Webb). His *Take the Lead* (with Betsy Myers) was named by Tom Peters and the *Washington Post* as Best Leadership Book of 2011.

Made in the USA
Columbia, SC
18 June 2020